Team Briefing and Beyond

A leader's guide to team meetings

Liz Cochrane and
Jenny Davenport

The Industrial Society

First published in 2001
The Industrial Society
Robert Hyde House
48 Bryanston Square
London W1H 2EA
Telephone: +44 (0)20 7479 2000

© The Industrial Society 2001

Reprinted: 2002
Ref: 5833JC.2.02

ISBN 1 85835 998 8

All rights reserved. No part of this publication may be reproduced, stored in a retrieval system or transmitted, in any form or by any means, electronic, mechanical, photocopying, recording and/or otherwise without the prior written permission of the publishers. This book may not be lent, resold, hired out or otherwise disposed of by way of trade in any form, binding or cover other than that in which it is published without prior written consent of the publishers.

Printed and bound in Great Britain by Formara Ltd

The Industrial Society is a Registered Charity no. 290003

Acknowledgements

With many thanks to the clients who shared their experiences with us over the years and to our colleagues at The Industrial Society who generously shared their knowledge of team meetings. In particular, we would like to thank Bob Shiers and Andrew Forrest for their feedback and suggestions on the booklet, and give our special thanks to Phil McGeough for his generosity in sharing his expertise in team meetings and in the tools and techniques of problem-solving. We couldn't have done it without you!

Contents

Acknowledgements — iii

Introduction — 1

1 **Different types of team meetings** — 5
   Meeting purpose — 5
   Tips for success in team meetings — 6

2 **The explaining meeting** — 14
   Advantages of the explaining meeting — 14
   Key pointers for the explaining meeting — 15

3 **The input meeting** — 24
   Advantages of an input meeting — 25
   Challenges of leading an input meeting — 26

4 **Team problem-solving** — 30
   Advantages of the problem-solving meeting — 30
   When to use problem-solving — 31
   Using team problem-solving — 31
   Problem-solving techniques — 35

Appendix 1 — 39
   Meeting planner

Further reading — 41

Introduction

This is a guide about how to conduct face-to-face team meetings.

Team meeting systems vary enormously in their aims and how they work in practice. Some (eg team briefing) are essentially mechanisms for keeping people in the picture and answering questions. Others encourage people to discuss relevant issues, think through local implications and contribute views and knowledge before decisions are taken; others involve people in problem-solving at organisation, division or team level. The Industrial Society has developed a 'spectrum' of meeting types to reflect this diversity.

This guide is for all leaders planning to run meetings for their teams, whether or not their organisation already runs a system. This might mean that some sections are irrelevant to you, but we hope that leaders will experiment with different ways of running meetings to best meet their team's needs – over and above any organisational requirements.

The Industrial Society has many years' experience supporting organisations in developing and running team briefing systems. This guide draws on that experience and goes further still – to look at how leaders can make the full spectrum of meeting types successful.

Chapter 1 looks at the different types of team meetings, and gives practical tips to help make meetings work effectively.

The remaining chapters look in more detail at each

meeting type, their benefits and how to make them successful.

Why communicate via meetings?

Communication makes the wheels of work turn. It's how we know what we have to do, and why. It's the way we transmit needs, knowledge, ideas. It's how we alert others to opportunities – and problems. It's how we influence; how we unleash creativity.

With constant change as the norm, communication has never been more important. More changes flounder because of poor communication than any other reason. Change creates stress, anxiety – and confusion. Without effective communication, performance drops along with morale. The grapevine flourishes. Speculation rules.

The information age means communication options have never been more varied: e-mail; intranet; voicemail; video and phone conferencing. Face-to-face meetings take time and resource, both to set up and to run. So why continue to invest in them?

Communication tools have different strengths and weaknesses. 'Lean' tools – such as e-mail – are invaluable for giving and exchanging information, facts and requests. But 'rich', face-to-face tools provide opportunities for dialogue where understanding can be checked, meaning explored, ideas developed, conflicts resolved, problems solved and relationships built. A key skill for everyone in the world of work today is to use the most appropriate communication tool – so, depending on your objectives, the additional time and effort involved in face-to-face communication can pay dividends.

Team-based communication has many benefits. For example, team briefings and other meetings can:

- build a sense of team
- ensure a joint focus and understanding of priorities and actions
- allow local meaning and implications of corporate information to be explored
- ensure team members know they have the same story
- provide opportunities to identify blocks to team performance, resolve problems and build on opportunities and successes
- enable differing views on issues affecting the team to be explored and resolved
- provide opportunities for team members to have their say on issues affecting them before decisions are taken
- create opportunities jointly to develop and build on ideas.

Numerous studies show face-to-face communication to be people's top choice. And recent research by The Industrial Society shows 90% of surveyed organisations see team briefings/team communication meetings as the most effective communication channel.

Chapter 1
Different types of team meetings

Most people have experience of meetings that progress in ever-decreasing circles. Typical results include:

- Stress from knowing that work is piling up.
- Frustration at listening to points of no interest or relevance.
- Anger from feeling that your contribution is ignored.

You want to make sure that your team meetings don't fall into this category.

Meeting purpose

There are very different purposes for different types of team meetings, or even for different parts of a meeting:

Explaining: Giving people information – especially that which builds team purpose or which may create an emotional response – and providing the opportunity for questions and feedback. Team briefing is a good example of this. Explaining meetings may also involve people discussing and reflecting on information that affects them, or concern new attitudes or behaviour the organisation would like to instil.

Gaining input: Consulting and gathering feedback on people's views and reactions to inform future decisions, ensure best quality decisions and encourage 'buy in'.

Problem-solving: Where issues are resolved and decisions taken. People need to know what the purpose of a meeting is, especially if you are moving from one purpose to another within the same meeting.

The remaining chapters look at the benefits of the different types of meetings, and how to make them successful. First, we will consider some best practice guidelines that apply no matter the meeting type.

Tips for success in team meetings

Principles

The principles of team briefing continue to hold good – and can be adapted for other meeting types. These include making sure that meetings are held:

Face-to-face: So that understanding can be checked, meaning explored, questions answered, feedback gathered and discussion generated, as appropriate.

In small teams: A team briefing (focusing on giving information and encouraging questions) works best in teams of between four and 15 people who share a common purpose. Larger than this and people become reluctant to ask questions. If you want to encourage team discussion and dialogue in a team meeting, a maximum size of eight works best. If your team is larger than this, think about splitting into sub-groups to discuss the implications of topics where you really want to get everyone to contribute.

On a regular basis: People can be suspicious of 'as and when' meetings – associating them with bad news. If you don't have an organisation-wide meeting system with frequency guidelines, decide how often to hold meetings on the basis of what you need to achieve through them. Whether you are using them for explaining and updating people, or getting their views and input, will the picture change weekly – or monthly? Agree a schedule of meetings at least six months in advance and stick to it.

About relevant subjects: Whether explaining, gaining input or problem-solving, you will not keep people's interest or motivation unless they can see the relevance to them. This means you need to think through how to ensure the team see the significance of any corporate topics. It also means taking time and care in thinking through the local input to the meeting. See Chapter 2 for practical tips.

With questions and feedback: As a minimum, it is important that people can ask questions, especially *why*. The benefits of other feedback, such as gathering views before decision taking, are discussed in Chapters 2 to 4.

Advance information
E-mail and intranets mean that communication is increasingly happening in 'real time' so team members

have access to information before a meeting. This is an *opportunity*, not a threat. Team meetings are still essential in creating true understanding. Use the time to:

- Draw attention to information people need to know. They may not have read it!
- Discuss team implications.
- Agree any actions required as a result of discussions.

Some meeting systems – such as team briefing – involve the leader introducing topics for the first time during the meeting, and talking through the team implications. A 'core brief' containing topics originating from senior managers and a 'local brief' prepared by the leader are used as prompts.

Other organisation-wide meeting systems may involve the advance distribution of core topics to everyone – via written or electronic media. This means team members come equipped to discuss what the item means for them, to share thoughts and responses, or agree actions.

You may also choose to circulate advance information on local items – for example, performance data or proposals for discussion. Doing this means people will be better prepared and more of the meeting time can be spent getting feedback and discussing implications and actions.

Guidelines to follow when considering giving information in advance:

- Make sure the team is ready for this style of meeting and understand their role in making it successful. Agreeing 'ground rules' to ensure effective dialogue can be beneficial: for example, getting joint

agreement that people will come prepared and will contribute what they know to discussion.
- Give information during the meeting rather than in advance where a topic is highly sensitive or requires a lot of context to manage concerns and build understanding.
- Check that people are both willing and able to access items beforehand. Keep reading matter clear and concise.
- Don't be tempted to circulate information and not discuss it. If you are not confident that 'core' information is relevant, raise this with your manager.
- Don't assume that everyone has read and understood! Start each item by asking a team member to summarise key points – use to check team understanding.
- Plan how to facilitate each item. Think of 'prompt' questions to encourage focused discussion.
- Manage the time required to discuss each item. Plan likely timings in advance and use to keep pace during the meeting.

The role of the meeting leader

Prepare the team meeting agenda

The best way to guarantee a return on the time the team invests in a meeting is to prepare in advance.

- Think through team items to include. Chapter 2 includes tips on selecting topics.
- It may be appropriate to provide team members with the opportunity to add agenda items. Check they are of genuine relevance to the whole team.

- Alert team members if you want them to play a specific role in the meeting or to lead one part of it.
- Where the meeting system includes corporate or divisional information (such as in team briefing), attend the meeting your manager leads. Use this to discuss and build your understanding of broader topics, and to ensure that you and your peers have a consistent interpretation. Think through how to make items relevant. Anticipate questions from your team. Ask the questions yourself to check your understanding. It is important that you and your peers give the same answer. Take notes – don't rely on memory.
- If you have difficulty seeing the relevance of a topic to your team, raise this as an issue. Your manager can help you find a way of making it relevant or agree to drop it.
- Take turns to share the main points of your local topics at your manager's meeting. People may want to add similar points in theirs. This serves as a useful channel of lateral communication.
- Once you have gathered your information, plan each agenda item. What are you aiming to achieve by including it? What meeting type should you use? Being clear will help get results.
- Plan the meeting structure. What is the logical sequence? People are most alert in the middle of a meeting, so place items needing maximum attention/input then. Don't artificially divide corporate and local topics – it's better if links can be drawn, to emphasise local meaning and relevance.
- Prepare any necessary presentation material.

A meeting planner is included in Appendix 1.

Different Types of Team Meetings

Organise the time and place
- Make sure that you have a quiet place where you will be uninterrupted and where seating allows all team members to have eye contact.
- Calculate the time needed for each item, and the meeting overall. This will vary according to the sort of team and the nature of the meeting. It may be as short as 20 minutes or as long as a day, depending on how often your team see each other in their day-to-day work, the degree of change to talk about and the extent to which views are sought or problems solved.
- Publish the agenda in advance via notice board or e-mail. Circulate advance information if appropriate.

Conducting the meeting itself – Organisation
- Begin on time.
- Note who is absent. Arrange for them to be brought up to speed later.
- If your organisation uses feedback sheets, ask a team member to record questions or other feedback on the form. If feedback is by e-mail or intranet, ask one of the team to take notes and send it off.
- If the meeting includes agreeing actions, decide how these will be captured. Make sure each action is allocated to an individual and has a deadline. Use at subsequent meetings to monitor progress.

Keep to time
- Announce the timetable at the beginning of the meeting, saying how much you have allocated for different items, or put the agenda on a flipchart.

- Ask a team member to act as timekeeper, giving updates and telling you and others when time for any item is running short.

Lead the meeting itself
- Be systematic: follow agenda items point by point.
- Make sure people are clear on the purpose of each item: for understanding, consultation, decision-taking?
- Allow time for questions and, where relevant, discussion. Summarise, then move on to the next item.
- At the end of the meeting, check there are no unanswered questions and that the person writing down questions, feedback for senior managers or actions has captured all points to everyone's satisfaction.
- Thank everyone for their time and contributions.

After the meeting
- Ensure feedback is sent off promptly. Follow through if necessary to ensure people receive a response.
- Deal with any issues that you promised to deal with.
- Ensure absentees are briefed.

Alternative meeting arrangements for dispersed teams
It may not be physically possible to get team members together for every team meeting. Consider use of 'live' conferencing via phone, video or e-mail. These have their own rules – for example, taking special care to explain things carefully given the lack of visual cues.

Don't overuse. Much of the value of a 'rich', face-to-face team meeting is lost when meetings are held electronically, so try to include opportunities to meet face-to-face at least quarterly.

Chapter 2
The explaining meeting

This is the meeting or part of a meeting where you are sharing progress, plans and news, explaining the rationale for a decision or repeating some information people already have to ensure common understanding.

A good explaining meeting both clarifies facts so that everyone has the same understanding and generates or responds to feelings to help create the energy for action.

Team briefing is one type of 'explaining' meeting, where the leader introduces items to the team, using the core brief plus locally prepared information, and provides opportunities for questions and feedback. Alternatively, 'explaining' meetings may be in the form of a team dialogue where the leader facilitates a discussion about items circulated in advance. Or they may be a mix of the two.

Advantages of the explaining meeting

- The team gains a common understanding of issues and decisions. When merely reading information via intranet, e-mails or publications, or even experiencing a senior management presentation, individuals are likely to have slightly different

interpretations of the implications for the team, if not the facts themselves. A team meeting can align people's views on the interpretation.
- People engage in the subject matter by talking it through for themselves. The process of discussion helps people to see things in different ways – increasing the likelihood of changed attitudes.
- People can ask questions or discuss implications in a small, safe environment where questions will be fully understood and the relevant team-level detail can be investigated.
- The organisation may want feedback on people's views and reactions to what is happening so that senior managers are more in touch. This can inform both future planning and communication.
- You can raise the issues which matter most to you about the way the team is going and how you want it to go. A recent Industrial Society survey found that enthusiasm is the single most important action people ascribe to effective 'leaders'. The explaining part of the meeting is where you can convey your enthusiasm and sense of purpose to your team.

Key pointers for the explaining meeting

Balance corporate and local information
The emphasis of explaining meetings should be on *local* information. As a rough guide, spend about two thirds of the time on this.

If the meeting includes topics that have originated

from senior managers, an important part of your role will be to help the team understand what each topic means for them. This means using the core brief as a prompt as you put each item into your own words, explain local implications then ask for questions. Where 'core' information is made available to the team in advance, your role becomes one of facilitation, encouraging dialogue, keeping it on track and capturing feedback. You may also need to add explanations where you have more knowledge than team members.

Identify appropriate topics

Think through topics with care – or the meeting will become overloaded. Communicate via face-to-face meetings where:

- It is important that everyone knows and understands the information and what it means for them (written information is easy to ignore/misinterpret).
- A topic will impact on the team or action is required from all team members.
- Common understanding will help 'build' the team and help it work towards its purpose.
- Real change is required in the way people think or behave – so that understanding the rationale and thinking the issue through is essential.
- Complex or sensitive information may otherwise be misinterpreted or cause concern.
- You know it is an issue that people are interested in or concerned about.
- You want to get people's views and feedback.

Other topic tips:
- Use team and organisational objectives to think if there is anything to say, anyone to congratulate, anything to ask people.
- Are there any recent incidents where you may want to remind people of rules or congratulate them?
- What is disturbing people? What's on the grapevine? Find out the latest information.
- Think about how to talk about performance (see below).
- Think about the coming month. What is coming up or what changes are you planning that you need to tell people about or ask their views? Be clear about when you are asking for views and when you are just informing people.
- What have you or the organisation communicated since the last team meeting? Never 'hoard' time sensitive information – people need it promptly. Consider whether expanding on it or talking about implications will deepen understanding.
- Review agendas and feedback from previous meetings – give updates as appropriate.
- Provide relevant updates from project or problem-solving teams.
- Whatever the topic, include *why* something is happening or planned, as well as the what, how and when. Building understanding of the reasons for decisions or actions is critical.
- Talk about both good and bad news. Be honest and positive with both: acknowledge problems and talk about what is being done to resolve them – or involve the team in discussing the way forward.

- Keep the agenda future focused. A minimum of 60% of the meeting should look forward.

Talking about performance

The key topic for almost every team meeting is performance. This is as true for the team working in the same office as for the team where members only come together for the team meeting.

It is important to give a sense of whether the team is succeeding, to praise those who have contributed most to recent success and to talk about what actions can be taken to consolidate success or avoid repetition of failure. The team meeting gives the team a sense of what is important in its work and what it is doing for the whole organisation. It provides focus and context for day-to-day activities and communication.

What you cover and the tone you use are therefore two essential aspects of your leadership. It is important to have some continuity in how you talk about performance. It is also helpful if there is an objective measure, rather than merely 'seems a bit better'. Here are some thoughts about how to decide what measures to use regularly:

- What is the purpose of the team, ie what does it do for the organisation?
- What is your personal key performance indicator which your manager most cares about?
- What measures do team members most influence by their individual performances?

There may not currently be any figures which measure your performance, especially for service departments. Perhaps you should create some, for example, measure internal customer satisfaction or the proportion of times you cannot meet a request from an internal customer. Involve your team as well as your manager and customers in working out what these measures might be.

There may also be measures which feature for a few months while you or the organisation are having a campaign about them.

Put yourself in the team's shoes

You understand your team, better than anyone else in the organisation. It is your job to put issues across or prompt a discussion in a way that will most interest them, and which draws out the meaning and implications for the team. The sorts of questions to ask yourself when preparing are:

- What is the team's current knowledge about this topic?
- What are their preconceptions or prejudices?
- How might they imagine this could affect them?
- How else might it affect them?
- What contacts do they have with other teams in the organisation which might be affected, and how will those other teams be affected?
- What might their fears or hopes be?
- With what other information might they associate this topic? What sorts of associations will that carry with it, eg they may remember a similar initiative some years ago and they might assume that this will have similar consequences?

Face the snags and down sides of your information

It is your job to put across the management view on a topic. There will almost certainly be contrary views, if only 'Why hasn't this been done earlier?' The most effective way of dealing with the flip sides of your case is to be frank about them and then to reiterate the reasons for the decision.

By being open about the snags yourself you can shut off unnecessary discussion.

What to do when you think the organisation has made a poor decision

This is a hard one. It is most unlikely in your whole career that there will never be a time when you do not have to explain or defend an unpopular decision, or one with which you personally disagree. It may seem more honest to be open about your reservations. In the long run, it does neither you nor the team any favours to criticise the organisation or its decisions. Your team know that it is part of your job as a manager to put across the management line. If you duck that then they will see you as having ducked your responsibilities, and will hold you in lower respect for it. There is always a case to be made for the management decision, no matter how poor you believe the decision to be. It is your job to stress this case and put across the reasons for the decision.

Where the decision is unpopular you may have to accept anger or sadness from your team. Think about what personal support you can enlist before and after the meeting to help you deal with this. Perhaps arrange to meet your mentor, if you have one, or a sympathetic colleague or your manager, to help you through your own inevitable feelings of hurt and anger.

Involve the team in explanations

Members of the team may be able to help with explanations. For example, some may be members of project teams which have worked on proposals now being communicated. Ask them to speak to that part of the meeting.

In other cases, people may have direct experience where they have a useful perspective to add. It shows how you notice and value the skills and experience you have in the team if you call on team members to present. Alert them in advance so that they can prepare and negotiate a time limit.

When thinking through with the team how a change might affect them, encourage everyone to speak. You may want to prime members of the team with particular experience in the topic.

Use visual aids

For many people being able to see something aids understanding. In particular, most people find it hard to take in layouts, figures or proportions when they are merely told them, while they will take on board a simple bar-chart or graph.

Looking at a flipchart, poster or screen also helps focus attention.

It is worth bearing in mind a few pointers:

- Keep visual aids simple with only a few words per screen.
- Give people time to read the information.

- Don't read the words out; talk people through the information.
- Talk to the team not to the visual aid.
- Check equipment before the meeting.
- Don't hide behind visual aids. The purpose of the meeting is for the team to talk not for you to present a lot of information.

Explain the news as stories
People love stories. Think of any presentation you attended recently. The parts you remember were almost certainly the stories. Facts and figures are meaningless unless constructed in some sort of story, with things being good or bad and having causes and effects.

Use examples
Use relevant examples. People find it easier to grasp these than generalities. In one case a clothing store supervisor was talking to her team about 'stock shrinkage'. She said 'We are losing £7,000 per day, or per week, or perhaps it was £70,000… well, it is the equivalent of someone nicking a pair of tights every 10 minutes'. No-one would have remembered the figure, even if she had got it right, but everyone took on board the example.

Avoid jargon
Good communication is clear and succinct. Talk about things in terms that the team will relate to. Jargon, acronyms and management-speak are best avoided. It is particularly easy to fall into this trap when sharing financial information. Translate it so that it is meaningful to all.

Value feedback

Encourage questions and feedback. Doing this helps check that the message understood is the same as the message sent. Understanding how people are thinking will also help you in your role as leader – and mean you will be even better placed to 'put yourself in your team's shoes' as you prepare for future meetings (see p. 19).

Effective preparation means you should be able to answer most questions on the spot. If not, never guess. Commit to getting an answer within a specific timescale (say 48 hours). Make sure you do so – even if it's to explain why a response isn't yet available and when it will be.

Avoid red herrings

Some people may raise issues or questions not on the agenda. While your response to this will depend on your relationship with the team, time management means it is best to stick to agenda items. Well planned agendas that give an opportunity to raise issues in advance help this. Agree to set aside team time to talk about other topics when everyone can be better prepared (including you).

Discuss issues affecting individuals during one-to-one's – don't take up team time.

Chapter 3
The input meeting

This is the meeting or part of a meeting where a decision has not yet been made but might be influenced by input from the meeting, as options are aired and points of view put forward.

Topics can be included at various stages of decision-making: from when a problem is first recognised and the meeting is asked questions to enable the decision-maker to understand the issue better, through every stage to where views are sought on a specific proposal before decision-taking.

The important thing is that people understand the aim that needs to be achieved, and why; any specific constraints (eg cost, time-scales, quality) and what is still open and what has already been decided. There is no need for consensus usually, since the decision will not be made at the meeting and the person taking the decision can absorb a range of views. People also need to understand that they are being consulted – so that their input is one of many factors the decision maker must consider before coming to a conclusion, rather than deciding what will happen.

The topic may be organisation-wide, or come from a project team, from you as the leader or from a member of the team wanting an issue aired before he or she takes a decision.

This is also the meeting or part of a meeting where you and your team can talk about what is working and what is not working so well. It is worth reserving time in meetings on a regular basis, perhaps once a quarter or once every six months at least, to ask the team what is working well in the team, that you can celebrate and build on, and what is getting in the way of the team achieving more. The items that are impeding you can either be fed back up the organisation, if it is equipped to act on them, or dealt with within the team by problem-solving techniques.

You may want to ask a team member to facilitate this part of the meeting – for example, if people know you have strong views on an issue and you think they may speak out more if you aren't there! If so, it is important to ensure that the individual has appropriate training in facilitating discussion.

Advantages of an input meeting

- Better decisions are taken. People will mention potential pitfalls or unintended consequences of a course of action and plans can be made to avoid them. The wide range of knowledge and experience in the group will be tapped.
- People can think things through for themselves. This is particularly important where a major change in behaviour or priorities is envisaged. People often don't really take things on board until they have done the reasoning for themselves.
- People feel involved in the decision-making process. People can live better with decisions they don't like

if they feel that their interests and views have at least been listened to and, where possible, the influence of their views seen in the final decisions.
- Subsequent communication can be better targeted, concentrating on the issues which mean most to specific audiences, and in particular acknowledging changes which have been made as a result of their input and explaining why other suggestions or inputs have been ignored.

Before asking for input, it is important to make sure that the decision has not already been made. If it has – don't ask. Building understanding of the topic and its context before asking for input is also vital. Without this, contributions may miss the mark and people will become frustrated.

Challenges of leading an input meeting

Challenge no 1 – Dominance by the people who know

People may come to the meeting with very different levels of prior knowledge on the topic. Some may dominate the discussion while others will not dare open their mouths.

What you can do about it
- To a certain extent this may be inevitable. People who care and are knowledgeable are bound to have a greater say than those who don't care or who have little relevant knowledge or experience.

- Encourage people to inform themselves. Make sure people know the topic is going to be discussed and know where to find relevant information. This is particularly important for new team members.
- Make sure more knowledgeable members of the team explain any jargon and reasons for their views in a way that informs others.

Challenge no 2 – Gasbags

Whether or not they know more, some people will be more wordy than others. Some will quote a myriad of examples and others will have bees in their bonnet which they release at every opportunity. Allowing these people to take more air-time than their views warrant risks boring everyone and wasting time.

What you can do about it
- Emphasise the importance of time.
- If someone always waffles, or you know they will bore everyone about a particular item, it may be worth taking them on one side before the meeting and asking them to allow others to have their say. You may need to spend some time outside the meeting listening to their views, especially if they are particularly well-informed by their experience or observations.
- You may need, politely but firmly, to shut the person up. This can often be done by summarising their views and then asking for others' opinions.

Challenge no 3 – People don't contribute

The opposite problem. Some or all of the team are not opening their mouths. This may be caused by cynicism if they feel they have been asked for views in the past and no-one has taken any notice.

It may also happen where people are not used to discussing issues where they are not taking the decision. Managers starting to run input meetings often find a high proportion of people will be silent and wait and see.

In cultures where the boss has always been expected to have the answers, people may be reluctant to speak until they have heard your views, and then only speak if they agree.

What you can do about it
- Prepare. Think through 'prompt' questions that will stimulate discussion. Use 'open' questions that require more than a yes/no answer.
- Acknowledge cynicism. Be clear about what has already been decided and what is still open to change. This means you can nip in the bud any unproductive conversations about the wisdom of decisions already made, which will inevitably have no effect and might confirm people's belief that the organisation is not listening.
- People may fear that questions are merely cosmetic and that nothing they could say will change the decision already envisaged. All you can do is acknowledge this fear and point out that if they do not express their views then they certainly will have no influence.
- Draw out people's experience. Where you know a shrinking violet has useful knowledge to share, ask them in advance so that they can prepare their

contribution. Or ask direct questions of people in the meeting.
- Live with silence. Don't be tempted to answer your own question, ask less open questions or guess responses. Someone will eventually answer. Build on this to encourage others to speak.
- Show that you are listening well and with respect. Demand others do the same. People are reluctant to speak if they feel belittled or embarrassed when they do. Don't allow yourself or other people to laugh at suggestions, or write them off by word or gesture. Truly creative ideas often sound daft initially.
- Keep a mental checklist of points made. Summarise at key moments to show they have been heard and to check your own understanding of what has been said.
- Use techniques like brainstorming and prioritising to manage the discussion. See the next chapter for a short outline of some useful techniques.
- Choose carefully when to state your views. Too early and you will stifle the contribution of others.
- Always make sure people know what has happened as a result of their feedback: finish the story. Confidence will grow as people see results.
- Get to know people outside the meetings. The stronger your relationship with them – and team members with each other – the more confident people will feel.
- Be patient and let the amount of discussion grow over the months.

Chapter 4
Team problem-solving

This is the meeting or part of a meeting where the team solves problems.

Of course, teams and individuals solve problems every day as part of their work. The problems that come to team meetings are usually, therefore, the knottier ones. Often they are linked to relationship difficulties, differences of opinion within the team, lack of role clarity or relations between your team and others.

Real problems like these need techniques to help solve them. These can enable the team to move out of the bind whereby the same thinking that created the problem won't find a solution for it.

Advantages of the problem-solving meeting

- Problems are solved, improving performance and eliminating frustration.
- Improvements in customer service, cost reduction, quality and other key 'bottom line' indicators.
- Use of problem-solving tools avoids wasted time and enhances meeting skills.
- Improved teamwork and interpersonal skills – listening in particular.
- Greater participation and ownership.

When to use problem-solving

- When an issue is raised in or outside the team meeting where a quick discussion will not get to the bottom of the topic or produce a full solution.
- The issue may well arise from the question about what is not working well in the team.
- When at least some of the expertise to solve the problem exists within the team.

Using team problem-solving

Training in the use of problem-solving tools helps people to use them easily and well. Here are some simple ground rules and techniques to get you started.

There is a logical sequence to problem-solving: problem identification, analysis and resolution.

1 Define the problem you are going to solve

Problems tend to link to each other. Also, team members may each have a slightly different idea of what the problem is. Before starting to break the problem down, or investigate its causes, it is essential to check that everyone has a clear idea of what the problem is.

Using a flipchart to note alternative ideas, get the group to define the problem that they are going to solve. This may take time, and you (and the team) may just want to get on with solving it. However, without this stage you risk having real problems with different interpretations later. Try to define the problem within boundaries that you yourselves can control, rather than, say, customer behaviour, which you can't.

It is easier to solve small problems than large ones, so breaking down a monster problem into bite-sized chunks and solving them one at a time may make sense. On the other hand, if it is really one large problem there is a danger that you will miss the complexities of it if you attempt to divide it up unnaturally.

2 Say what having solved the problem will look like

This, in a way, is a check on the first process. It verifies that the team all have the same idea of the problem and tells the team when it has done enough to solve the problem. It helps if the desired end state is measurable.

3 Don't reinvent the wheel

If your organisation runs some sort of register of problem-solving teams, perhaps on the intranet or via the quality department, register your team and its project. If there is a good register of successful projects it would be worth checking whether there is some practice already operating in another part of the organisation which would solve your problem.

Even if there is not a register of projects there may be a best practice exchange of some sort which you could check, or you may be able to approach others informally where you think they may have some useful experience.

4 Decide what team should solve it

Sometimes the whole team can solve a problem, and you can hold the problem-solving session as part or the whole of a team meeting. More often, the problem-solving team will need to be a sub-team, often involving one or more people from outside your team. It is particularly important to include members of other teams if it seems likely that they will need to change to implement the solution.

The criteria for choosing the team members should be:

- Keenness to solve the problem.
- Open-mindedness about the cause and likely solution to the problem.
- Willingness to contribute to the group and genuinely listen to other people's contributions.
- Some relevant knowledge to solving it. This will not necessarily be experience of the problem or its effects, but may be from having worked on a similar problem or having some specialist knowledge which might be relevant.
- No more than eight or nine people, preferably five or six.
- At least one person (to lead or facilitate it) with a good knowledge of problem-solving techniques. This may be you, but it is good if you delegate the leadership of problem-solving groups to others.
- People who have not yet had a chance to serve on a team should be included when possible, to spread the knowledge and habit of problem-solving.

5 Investigate the problem

Use cause and effect analysis (see p. 36) to get to the bottom of the issue. Once the real problem is identified, collect evidence by allocating individual investigative work to team members.

6 Quantify the scale of the problem

Some problems prove to be inconsequential once preliminary investigation is complete. Don't waste valuable time resolving minor issues. Find relevant facts and figures to enable you to size the issue. What is the problem costing? How widespread is it? What patterns are emerging?

The use of pareto analysis is useful at this stage. If there are no statistical skills in your team you may want to enlist some help.

7 Choose corrective action

Brainstorming can be helpful in thinking creatively about the options open to you.

Sometimes there is one compelling solution. More likely, teams are faced with options. These need to be examined and tested. Don't rush to solutions: evaluate each in terms of impact, cost, resources and simplicity.

8 Implement corrective action

If all the resources needed to solve the problem are within your authority, you can simply implement the corrective action.

The team may need to put together a case for spending money to resolve the problem. This will require a cost benefit analysis, and again they may need help if they don't have the necessary skills within the team.

If the solution also requires change from another department or team, talk through with the team how best to present the issue. If the likelihood of another team needing to change can be anticipated, ask a representative to join the team as early as possible.

9 Monitor corrective action

Once corrective action has been taken, you or the team need to monitor to ensure that it has the desired effect. If it does not, ask the team to review the problem again. Don't disempower them by taking another decision or returning to the old way of doing things without consulting them.

10 Recognise the achievement

There may be some organisation-wide scheme for publicising and congratulating teams. If not, celebrate the achievement during a team meeting or arrange a special team event.

Make sure the team keeps records of their analyses at each stage of problem-solving, for use in other problem-solving by your team on another occasion or for other teams.

Problem-solving techniques

This is a very quick summary of some key problem-solving techniques, with suggestions of others that are in common use (See Further Reading for books on problem-solving). It is really important that facilitators, and in some cases everyone, are trained in these techniques.

Problem identification tools

Brainstorming

In fact, this technique can be used at various stages, in both problem identification and in thinking of solutions.

The leader defines the issue and invites the team to suggest ideas, which are then recorded on a flipchart.

Rules of brainstorming:

1 No judgements are made about suggestions.
2 All ideas, however wacky, are welcomed.
3 The more ideas the better.
4 Ideas can be refined, combined and piggybacked.

At the end of the first phase, the team takes a short break and then returns to critique the ideas.

Other tools commonly used to identify problems include **theme analysis** and **paired comparisons**.

Problem analysis tools

Cause and effect analysis

A 'why-why' chart helps the team identify the real causes of problems:

1 State the problem on the left-hand side of the paper.
2 Create a 'tree' of causes to the right of the problem by asking a succession of 'whys' regarding the problem and each of the possible causes.
3 Continue this process until a sufficient level of detail has been achieved.

Pareto analysis and **fishbone technique** are also valuable tools at this stage.

Problem resolution tools

Force field analysis

This is a useful technique when getting to the stage of planning implementation, especially if you are looking for people to change their behaviour.

Force field analysis shows the relative strength of the forces for change and the restraining forces. The more you push change the stronger the restraining forces become. The most effective way of achieving change is therefore to diminish the strength of the restraining forces:

1 List the forces for change.
2 List the restraining forces.
3 Think of ways to diminish the strength of the restraining forces.

Problem rectification analysis can also be helpful during this stage as can **brainstorming** and **paired comparisons**.

Appendix 1
Meeting planner

Topic	Who will lead	Type of item: – Explaining – Input – Problem-solving/ Decision-taking

Further reading

101 Creative Problem Solving Techniques, James M Higgins, New Management Publishing Co, 1883629004

Effective Problem-Solving, Steven Kneeland, How To Books, 1857033515

How To Be A Better Problem Solver, Michael Stevens, Kogan Page 0749419016